Craft Lacing

Madness

Craft Lacing

Madness

Francine Fittes

D&C

David and Charles

For my mother, herself a great scoubidou maker.
For Laurent, Denis and Mimiblonblon
for their unfailing support, and for everyone I love.

A DAVID & CHARLES BOOK
This edition copyright © David & Charles Limited 2005

David & Charles is an F+W Publications Inc. company
4700 East Galbraith Road
Cincinnati, OH 45236

First published in the US in 2005
First published in the UK in 2005 as *Scoubidou Madness*

First published in France as *Scoubidou Folies* in 2003
Text and illustrations copyright © Fleurus 2003

Francine Fittes has asserted her right to be identified as author of this work in accordance
with the Copyright, Designs and Patents Act, 1988.

A catalogue record for this book is available from the British Library.

ISBN 0 7153 2480 2 paperback (US only)

Printed in China by SNP Leefung
for David & Charles
Brunel House   Newton Abbot   Devon

The author and publisher have made every effort to ensure that all the instructions in this
book are accurate and safe, and therefore cannot accept liability for any resulting injury,
damage or loss to persons or property however it may arise.

Visit our website at www.davidandcharles.co.uk

David & Charles books are available from all good bookshops; alternatively you can
contact our Orderline on 0870 9908222 or write to us at FREEPOST EX2 110, D&C Direct,
Newton Abbot, TQ12 4ZZ (no stamp required UK only); US customers call 800-289-0963
and Canadian customers call 800-840-5220.

Enter the wacky world of craft lacing with these crazy and colorful projects!

Craft lacing (also known as Boondoggle and Scoubidou) is a fast and fun way to create funky forms. By bending, weaving, knotting and making all kinds of special moves with the craft-lacing threads (also known as scoubidou threads), you can transform them into dozens of weird and wonderful shapes. You can buy the threads in many toy and craft stores.

Follow the simple basic techniques shown, and become an expert in no time! Then move on to the brilliant projects to create over 30 animals and figures to keep yourself or to give away as cool gifts.

Contents

6   **The basics**
9   **Classic techniques**

The projects

16 **Party napkin rings**

18 **Octopus magnets**

20 **Stick men**

22 **Funny faces**

24 **Greedy lizard**

26 **Grasshopper and friends**

28 **Celebrate nature!**

32 **Animal parade**

38 **Keyring zing**

40 **Martian buddies**

42 **Fantasy beasts**

The basics

Scoubidou threads

There are three different types of scoubidou thread: hollow, solid, and flat. They usually come pre-cut ready for you to use in 90cm (36in) strands. You can use any of these for making classic scoubidous.

Scoubidous are usually made with 45cm (18in) strands plaited together. Depending on your choice of starting knot, you will either fold or cut your threads in half.

Scoubidou threads can be reinforced. You can do this by inserting lengths of wire into hollow threads.

Basic tool kit
- scissors
- glue
- wire (approx 0.7mm/$\frac{1}{36}$in in diameter)
- old scissors
- pencil
- wooden spoon or large felt-tip pen
- toothpicks and a wooden skewer

Be careful!
Cut wire with a pair of old scissors to avoid injury.

Starting off your scoubidou

Standard knot
45cm (18in) scoubidou threads are the most commonly used. Tie them in a knot at one end.

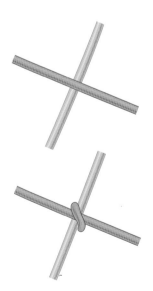

Hidden knot
Cross 2 lengths of 90cm (36in) thread at their centres. Knot one thread around the other. When plaiting 6 or more strands, use one thread to tie the others together at their centre.

Loops

Single loop: Tie a length of thread around a pen at its centre. Make another loose knot. Thread the other thread or threads through the loop. Tighten. Remove the pen after several rows.

Double loop: To make a 4-strand scoubidou, take 2 x 90cm (36in) threads and fold in half. Make a knot with both threads at the same time.

Holding knot

Bundle the strands together and tie with a spare end of thread. When the scoubidou is finished, remove this thread. Trim the other threads close to your work.

Finishing off your scoubidou

Simple fastening
Pull your last row tight, then trim the ends close to your work.

Rounded fastening
Finish 4-strand scoubidous by knotting 2 threads diagonally. Tighten. Knot the other 2 threads and trim. Finish 6-strand scoubidous by knotting the central threads as per 4-strand scoubidous. Then knot the other 2 threads.

Reinforcing

Reinforcing thread
Insert a length of wire into a hollow scoubidou strand.

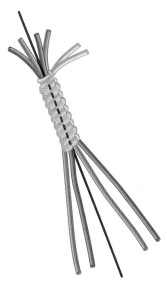

Reinforcing your scoubidou work
Before you pull your work tight, thread a length of wire into your starting knot, leaving 1–2cm (⅜–¾in) excess. Plait your Scoubidou around the wire. To avoid injury, push a piece of putty onto each end or wrap some sticky tape around them.

Before you begin...

Here are some handy techniques you will need for the projects.

Front hole

This makes it easier to insert wires into your scoubidou. Begin your scoubidou with a holding knot. Plait it for 2 or 3 rows around a toothpick with the sharp ends cut off.

Spacer row

Use this to create spaces in your scoubidou. Depending on the size of the space you need you could use a pen, the handle of a wooden spoon or a large felt-tip pen. Where you need a spacer, hold the object on the scoubidou and plait 2 successive rows before taking it out.

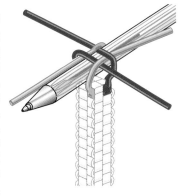

Holes

Use a wooden toothpick with the sharp ends cut off. Work in the same way as for a spacer row, inserting the toothpick where you need a hole.

Finishing threads

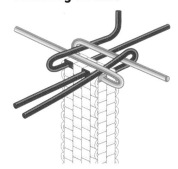

Simply trim 2 strands close to your work and continue to work your scoubidou with the new number of threads.

Adding threads

Before pulling your rows tight, slide the new threads into the loops you have made, leaving approx 2cm (¾in) excess. Plait 2 or 3 rows around them, then trim them. Carry on plaiting as normal.

Gluing

Use a solvent-free, all-purpose glue. Hold glued parts in place with clothes pegs or rubber bands. Leave to dry out thoroughly.

Classic techniques

3-strand scoubidou

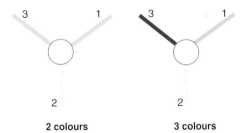

2 colours	3 colours

1 Tie a standard knot using 45cm (18in) threads. Separate the threads out and arrange them as shown in the diagrams.

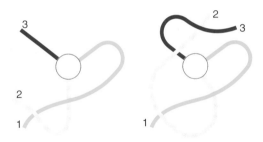

2 Cross thread 1 under thread 2 and let go, then cross thread 2 under thread 3 and let go.

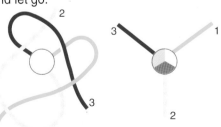

3 Pass thread 3 through the loop in thread 1. Pull this first row tight. Arrange the threads as at step 1. Continue in this way until you reach your desired length.

4-strand square scoubidou

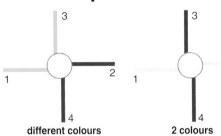

different colours	2 colours

1 Taking 2 x 90cm (36in) threads, start by making a loop or hidden knot. Arrange the threads as shown in the diagrams.

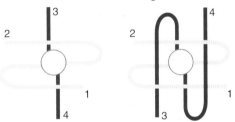

2 Make 2 loops with 2 opposite threads. Pass the remaining 2 threads into the loops.

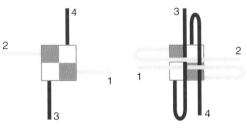

3 Pull this first row tight. Repeat until you reach your desired length.

9

4-strand round scoubidou

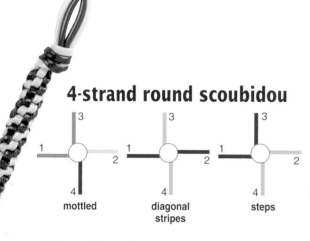

| mottled | diagonal stripes | steps |

1 Depending on the number of colours you want to use and the knot you have chosen, use 2 x 90cm (36in) threads divided in half, or 4 x 45cm (18in) threads. Arrange the threads according to your desired pattern.

2 Plait your first row in the same way as for the square scoubidou. Pull tight.

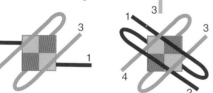

3 Lay 2 threads diagonally, as shown in the diagram. Plait.

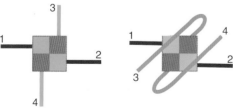

4 Tighten and repeat until you reach your desired length.

Rectangular scoubidou (6 or 8 strands)

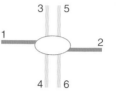

sides and edges in the same colour with 6 strands

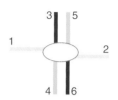

centre strip with 6 strands

1 Select 3 or 4 threads 90cm (36in) in length. Start off with a loop or hidden knot. Arrange the threads according to the pattern you want to make.

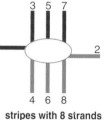

stripes with 8 strands

2 Make 2 loops over the knot with threads 1 and 2.

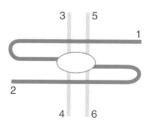

3 Plait your scoubidou with your remaining 4 or 6 threads.

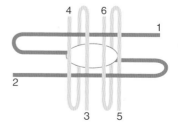

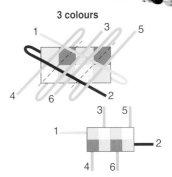

3 colours

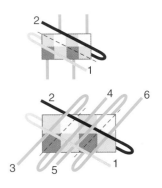

6-strand spiral

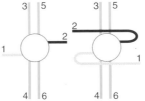

1 Knot 1 black thread and 1 white thread, then attach 2 blue threads in their centre, as for the single loop. Arrange the threads as shown in the diagram.

4 Plait the other threads in pairs, following the diagonal of each of the squares. Tighten.

2 colours

4 Tighten. 6 threads will give you a rectangle with 8 small coloured squares. 8 threads will give you 12 squares.

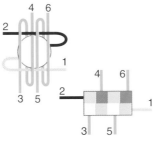

2 First row: follow the method for the rectangular scoubidou (steps 2, 3 and 4).

5 Third row: place threads 1 and 2 along the diagonal of the rectangle. Plait the other threads diagonally, two at a time.

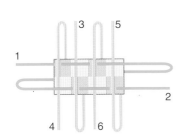

5 Make another 2 loops with threads 1 and 2, then plait the other threads. Tighten. Repeat from step 2 until you reach your desired length.

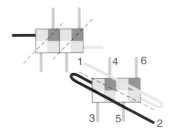

3 Second row: divide up your work into 2 squares, each made up of 4 small squares. Lay thread 1 and thread 2 along the diagonal of the rectangle.

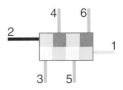

6 Tighten your threads. They should be back in the position you started in. Repeat steps 3, 4 and 5 until you reach your desired length.

8- or 10-strand spiral

These work on the same principle as the 6-strand spiral.

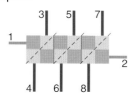

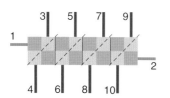

Plaiting is divided into 3 squares for an 8-strand spiral and 4 squares for a 10-strand spiral.

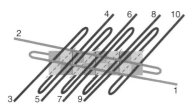

Place threads 1 and 2 along the diagonal of the rectangle. Plait the remaining threads in pairs on the diagonal of each square.

8-strand square scoubidou

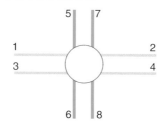

1 To make a two-toned scoubidou, take 2 x 90cm (36in) threads in each of your 2 chosen colours. Start by making a loop or hidden knot. Arrange the threads as shown in the diagram.

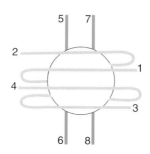

2 Make 4 loops with threads 1, 2, 3 and 4.

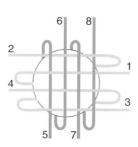

3 Weave threads 5, 6, 7 and 8, pulling them tight as you go.

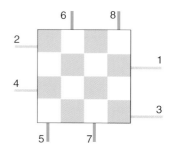

4 Tighten and check the position of your threads. You should have a check pattern of 16 small coloured squares.

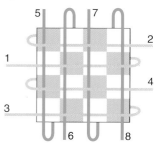

5 Make another 4 loops with threads 1, 2, 3 and 4, then plait the other threads. Pull tight. Repeat from step 2 until you reach your desired length.

8-strand round scoubidou

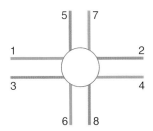

1 To make a two-toned scoubidou, take 2 x 90cm (36in) threads in each of your 2 chosen colours. Start by making a loop or hidden knot. Arrange your threads as shown in the diagram.

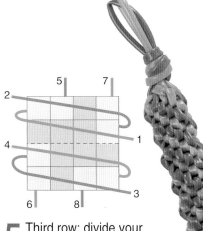

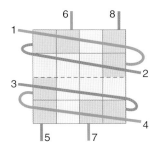

3 Second row: divide your work into 2 horizontal rectangles. Place threads 1 and 2 along the diagonal of the first, and threads 3 and 4 along the diagonal of the second rectangle.

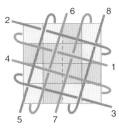

5 Third row: divide your work up into 2 horizontal rectangles. Place threads 1 and 2 over the diagonal of the first, then threads 3 and 4 along the diagonal of the second rectangle.

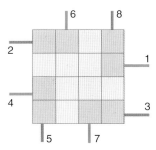

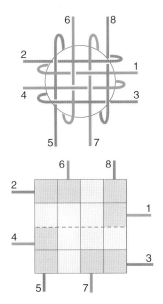

2 First row: proceed as for the 8-strand square scoubidou (steps 2, 3 and 4).

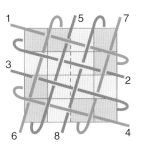

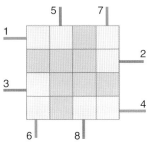

4 Divide your work into 2 vertical rectangles. Weave threads 5 and 6, then 7 and 8, along their diagonals. Tighten.

6 Divide your work into 2 vertical rectangles. Weave your remaining threads in pairs along their diagonals.

7 Pull tight. Repeat steps 3 to 7 until you reach your desired length.

13

The
Projects

Party napkin rings

You will need...

- 4 x 90cm (36in) scoubidou threads in one colour or 4 assorted colours
- 2 x 10mm (⅜in) wooden beads
- offcuts of foam board
- pen
- scissors
- glue

2 Untie your holding knot. Thread your scoubidou back through the spacer row to make a loop.

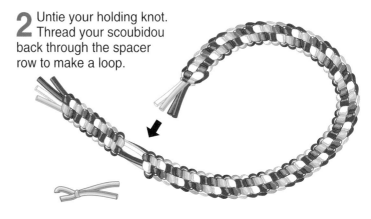

3 Trim your threads, leaving 1.5cm (⅝in) excess at each end of 2 of your threads. Apply a little glue to the threads. Thread them into your beads.

4 Using the templates at the back of this book, cut out a head and hat from foam board. Stick them onto your napkin ring. Add hands to make a place name card.

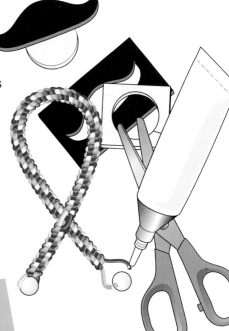

1 Tie your 4 threads together with a holding knot 1.5cm (⅝in) from their ends. Start by making a round scoubidou. At 17cm (6¾in), make a spacer row around a pen (see p.8). Continue the scoubidou over 2cm (¾in).

Tip
Make sure the holes in your beads are big enough to accommodate your scoubidou thread.

Bon appétit!

Octopus magnets

You will need...
- 6 x 45cm (18in) scoubidou threads, 4 threads for your main colour and 2 threads in another colour
- wire
- moving eyes
- 1 round magnet
- glue
- scissors
- old scissors
- wooden skewer or pen

1 Tie your 6 threads 5cm (2in) from their ends with a holding knot. Weave a rectangular scoubidou over 2cm (¾in). Separate the threads into 2 matching groups. Weave 2 scoubidous, each with 3 threads, over 5cm (2in).

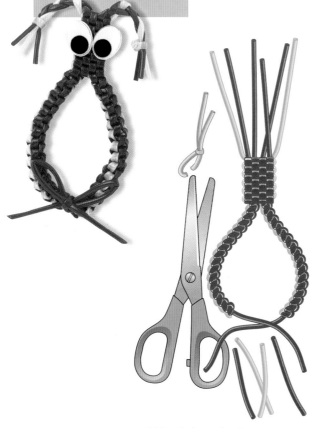

2 Trim 2 threads close to your work on each scoubidou. Tie the remaining threads. Untie your holding knot.

Plaits
Plait your threads and tie them together with an end of thread.

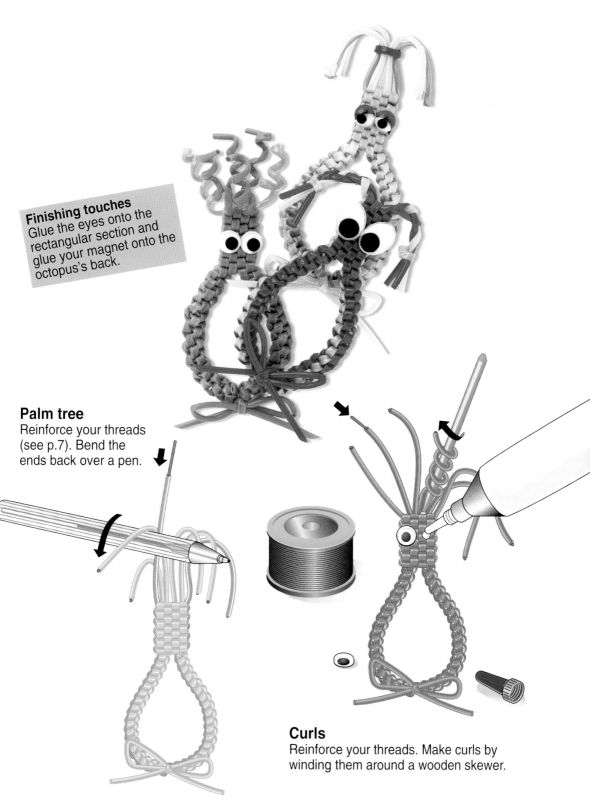

Finishing touches
Glue the eyes onto the rectangular section and glue your magnet onto the octopus's back.

Palm tree
Reinforce your threads (see p.7). Bend the ends back over a pen.

Curls
Reinforce your threads. Make curls by winding them around a wooden skewer.

19

Stick men

You will need...
- 1 x 20mm (¾in) pompom
- marker pen and scissors

To make one orange and green stick man:
- 45cm (18in) scoubidou threads: 5 orange, 2 blue, 1 green

To make one red stick man:
- scoubidou threads:
  1 x red (90cm/36in);
  2 x red (45cm/18in);
  2 x white (45cm/18in);
  1 x pink (45cm/18in)
- large-holed buttons:
  1 large and 4 small

To make one pink stick man:
- scoubidou threads:
  1 x blue (90cm/36in);
  4 x pink (45cm/18in);
  1 x purple (45cm/18in)
- 1 small bell

2 Continue your scoubidou for 4.5cm (1¾in), adding 2 lengths of green thread at 1cm (⅜in) and 4cm (1½in). Finish with a rounded fastening (see p.7). Trim your starting threads close to your work.

3 Slide the remaining orange thread into your spacer row. Insert the pompom then knot the thread. Tie knots to form the arms and legs. Trim your threads to the required length.

1 Tie 2 blue threads and 4 orange threads together with a holding knot. Start by making a spiral scoubidou. After 2 rows, make a spacer row (see p.8) around a marker pen.

Variations
Halve a 90cm (36in) length of thread and make a loop. Thread on a button or bell. Tie on the other threads. Start a spiral or rectangular scoubidou. Proceed as for the orange and green man.

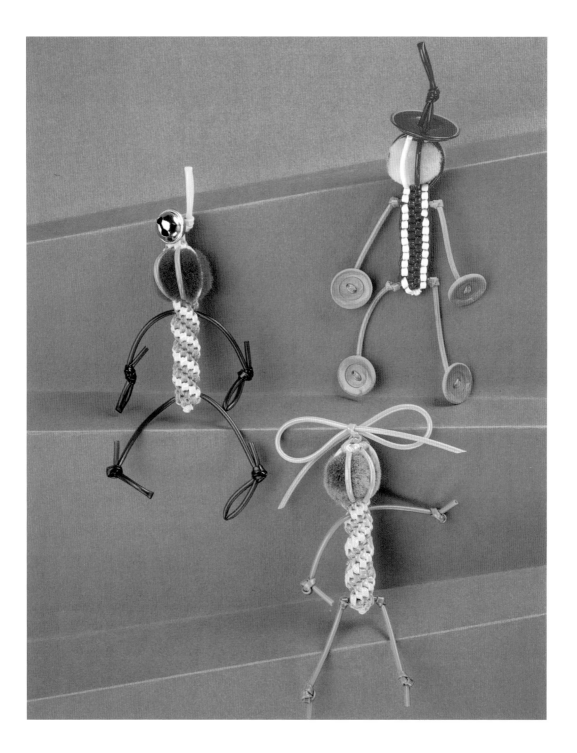

Funny faces

You will need...

- scoubidou threads:
  2 x 90cm (36in) threads in different colours, 2 x 8cm (3in) thread for the ears, 18cm (7in) for the glasses
- toothpick
- wire
- old scissors
- white card
- moving eyes
- sequins or pompom, 10mm (⅜in) in diameter (optional)
- glue

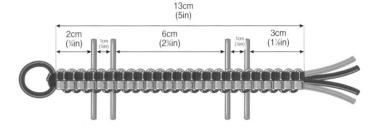

13cm (5in)

2cm (¾in) | 1cm (⅜in) | 6cm (2⅜in) | 1cm (⅜in) | 3cm (1⅛in)

1 Make a single loop in the middle of the 90cm (36in) threads. Start by weaving a round or square 4-strand scoubidou. At 2cm (¾in), make a spacer row (see p.8), then 3 more spacer rows as shown in the diagram.

2 At 13cm (5in), trim 2 threads down. Tie the 2 remaining threads. Pull tight. Make a loop.

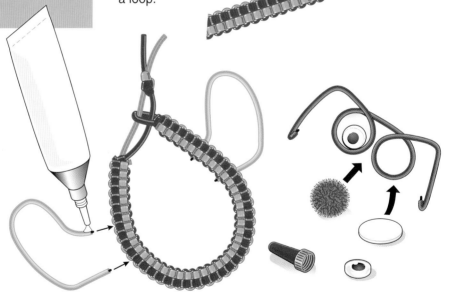

Tip If you find that you run out of thread, add more strands by following the instructions on page 8.

3 Reinforce the threads to make the ears and glasses (see p.7). Apply a little glue to the ears and insert them into the holes. Bend the scoubidou and insert the end into the first loop.

4 Make up the glasses. Stick a card circle behind each loop, then glue on the eyes. Secure the glasses behind the ears by bending them over. Glue on a pompom to make a nose.

Greedy lizard

You will need...
- 90cm (36in) scoubidou threads: 4 green, 2 yellow, 1 pink
- wire
- toothpick
- offcut of pink foam board
- moving eyes
- 2 round magnets
- glue
- old scissors
- scissors

2 Start by making a rectangular reinforced scoubidou with stripes. Make a spacer row at 2.5cm (1in) and another 4.5cm (1¾in) after that. Continue weaving for 1.5cm (⅝in).

3 Reduce your thread numbers by 2 green threads. With your 4 remaining threads and the wire, continue weaving a round scoubidou for 6cm (2⅜in).

4 Trim your wire close to your work, then finish with a rounded fastening. Untie your holding knot. Trim all threads.

Tip
Read pages 6 to 8 very carefully.

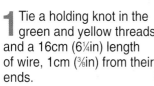

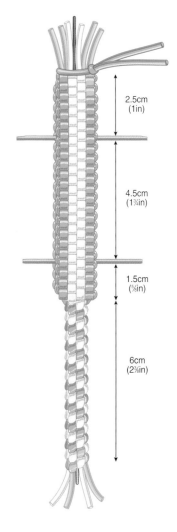

2.5cm (1in)

4.5cm (1¾in)

1.5cm (⅝in)

6cm (2⅜in)

1 Tie a holding knot in the green and yellow threads and a 16cm (6¼in) length of wire, 1cm (⅜in) from their ends.

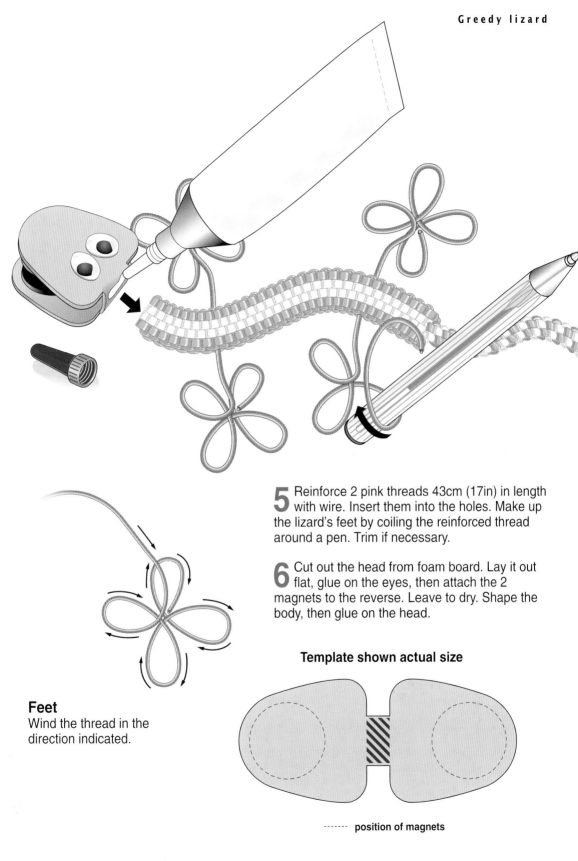

5 Reinforce 2 pink threads 43cm (17in) in length with wire. Insert them into the holes. Make up the lizard's feet by coiling the reinforced thread around a pen. Trim if necessary.

6 Cut out the head from foam board. Lay it out flat, glue on the eyes, then attach the 2 magnets to the reverse. Leave to dry. Shape the body, then glue on the head.

Template shown actual size

Feet
Wind the thread in the direction indicated.

------- **position of magnets**

Grasshopper and friends

You will need...
- 1 wooden bead 20mm (¾in) in diameter
- toothpick
- wire and old scissors
- glue
- scissors

To make the grasshopper:
- body: 1 x 90cm (36in) dark green thread and 2 x 90cm (36in) light green thread
- feet: 50cm (20in) light green thread

To make the cricket:
- body: 1 x 90cm (36in) each of lilac and purple thread; 1 x 45cm (18in) each of black and white thread
- feet: 45cm (18in) black thread

To make the fire bug:
- body: 2 x 90cm (36in) red thread and 1 x 90cm (36in) black thread
- feet: 45cm (18in) black thread

Grasshopper

1 Make up a 6-strand spiral scoubidou, starting from a single loop made using a toothpick (see p.7).

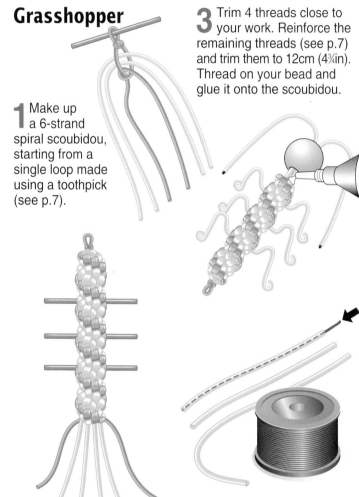

2 Make a hole with a toothpick at 1.5cm (⅝in), then 2 further holes 1cm (⅜in) apart (see p.8). Continue over 5cm (2in).

3 Trim 4 threads close to your work. Reinforce the remaining threads (see p.7) and trim them to 12cm (4¾in). Thread on your bead and glue it onto the scoubidou.

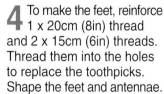

4 To make the feet, reinforce 1 x 20cm (8in) thread and 2 x 15cm (6in) threads. Thread them into the holes to replace the toothpicks. Shape the feet and antennae.

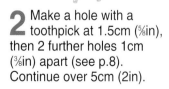

Cricket

Follow the same method as for the grasshopper, securing the two 45cm (18in) lengths in your starting knot. Make up the feet using 3 reinforced threads 15cm (6in) in length.

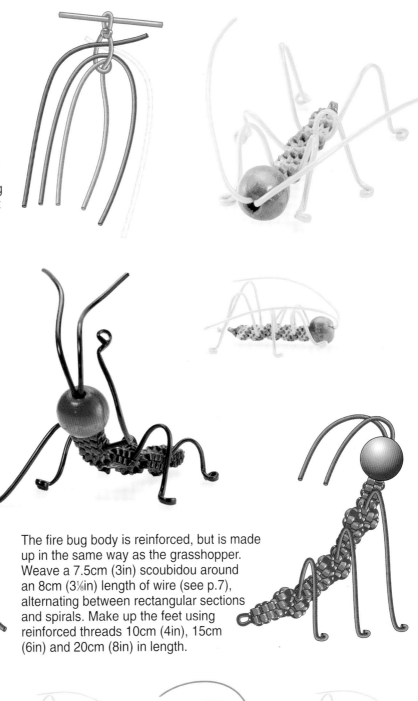

Fire bug

The fire bug body is reinforced, but is made up in the same way as the grasshopper. Weave a 7.5cm (3in) scoubidou around an 8cm (3⅛in) length of wire (see p.7), alternating between rectangular sections and spirals. Make up the feet using reinforced threads 10cm (4in), 15cm (6in) and 20cm (8in) in length.

Celebrate nature!

You will need...

To make one dragonfly:
- 90cm (36in) scoubidou threads in 3 different colours; 27cm (11in) transparent thread
- 2 beads 15mm (⅝in) and 20mm (¾in) in diameter
- glue
- wire
- old scissors
- sewing thread
- scissors
- moving eyes

Dragonfly

1 Thread a 38cm (15in) length of wire into your transparent scoubidou thread. Bend the covered end back.

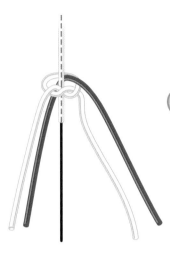

2 Weave a 4-strand round scoubidou around your transparent thread and wire, starting from a hidden knot 25cm (10in) from the covered end.

3 After 4.5cm (1¾in), thread on the small bead. Complete 2 rows.

4 Make up the wings using 2 threads 26cm (10¼in) and 30cm (12in) in length. Tie them together with sewing thread. Thread on the small wings. Complete a row as normal. Thread on the larger wings. Complete a row.

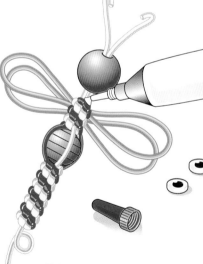

5 Trim any excess thread from the wings, and trim 2 scoubidou threads. Reinforce the antennae. Thread on the remaining bead and glue it onto the scoubidou. Glue on the eyes. Loop the covered wire under the abdomen.

Celebrate nature!

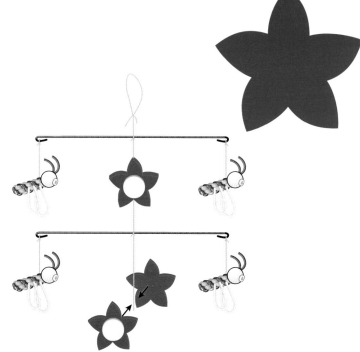

You will need...

To make one bee:
- 45cm (18in) scoubidou threads, 1 yellow, 1 black, 1 white
- 1 bead 15mm (⅝in) in diameter
- sewing thread
- wire
- moving eyes

To make the mobile and flowers:
- foam board in yellow and red
- 2 metal rods 20cm (8in) in length
- glue
- nylon thread
- old scissors
- scissors

Bee mobile

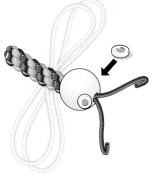

1 To make a bee, weave a 4-strand round scoubidou, starting from a hidden knot. Follow the same method as for the dragonfly. Thread on 2 pairs of wings made from one 18cm (7in) thread and one 20cm (8in) thread. Finish off the head.

2 To make the mobile: attach 4 bees to the metal rods with nylon thread. Cut 4 flowers out of foam board and glue them in pairs onto the centre thread.

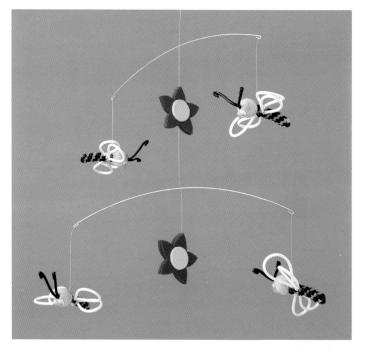

Snail

You will need...
- 45cm (18in) scoubidou threads, 4 green, 2 white, 1 orange
- 2 pompoms 8mm (5⁄16in) in diameter and 1 pompom 30mm (1⅛in) in diameter
- moving eyes
- wire
- old scissors
- scissors
- glue

1 Tie the green and white threads together with a holding knot 3cm (1⅛in) from their ends and weave a rectangular scoubidou over 6cm (2⅜in). Reduce your thread numbers by 2 green threads and continue weaving a square scoubidou over 2.5cm (1in). Finish with a rounded fastening (see p.7).

2 Cut the orange thread in half. Start by making a loop and weave a round scoubidou for 2 rows. Make a spacer row (see p.8), then complete another row. Pass the threads around the body. Complete another 2 rows. Trim the threads close to your work.

3 To make the head, trim 4 threads and reinforce the remaining 2. Glue a pompom and an eye onto each antenna.

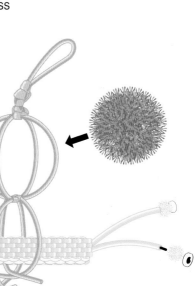

Animal parade

You will need...
- wire
- scissors
- old scissors
- moving eyes
- glue

To make one mouse:
- scoubidou threads:
  4 x 90cm (36in) threads in
  white, grey or black;
  1 x 22cm (8⅝in) pink thread

To make the cat:
- 45cm (18in) scoubidou
  threads, 4 orange and
  4 black
- toothpick
- wooden skewer

Mouse

Body
Reinforce a 12cm (4¾in)
length of pink thread. Attach
the 4 threads for the body
8cm (3¼in) from the end of
the tail with a hidden knot.
Weave a round scoubidou
around the reinforced
thread for 1cm (⅜in).

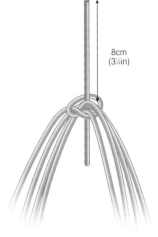

8cm
(3¼in)

Head
Make the ears with a 10cm (4in)
length of reinforced pink thread.
Thread them into the next row.
Reduce the number of threads
by 2 threads. Continue for
4 rows in a spiral. Reduce the
number of threads again and
complete a last row as for a
4-strand round scoubidou.
Finish with a rounded fastening.

1cm
(⅜in)

Finishing touches
Make the tail and nose by
shaping the end of the pink
thread. Glue on the eyes.

Tip
Read pages 6 to 8 very
carefully when making
any of these animals.

Cat

Hind paws

Tie 2 orange threads, 2 black threads and a 10cm (4in) length of wire with a holding knot 1cm (⅜in) from their ends. Make a round reinforced scoubidou over 2.5cm (1in). Make up a second identical scoubidou.

Body

Bring the 2 scoubidous together. Insert a 13cm (5in) length of wire in the centre, leaving 8cm (3¼in) excess for the tail. Weave a round reinforced scoubidou with the 8 threads. Once you reach 2cm (¾in), leave out the central wire, then continue for 0.5cm (³⁄₁₆in).

Front paws

Separate the threads and make 2 separate 4-strand round reinforced scoubidous for 2.5cm (1in). Trim all your threads close to your work.

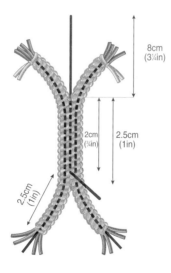

8cm (3¼in)

2cm (¾in)   2.5cm (1in)

2.5cm (1in)

Head

Tie 3 orange threads, 3 black threads and a toothpick together with a holding knot. Complete 2 rows in a spiral. Take out the toothpick. Trim your starting threads. Place your scoubidou onto the wire sticking out of the body. Weave for 1cm (⅜in). Make up the ears with a 6cm (2⅜in) reinforced orange thread and thread them into the next row.

Complete another row. Reduce your number of threads by 2 threads. Complete 2 rows as for a round scoubidou. In the next row, add 2 black threads 3cm (1⅛in) in length for the whiskers. Finish with a rounded fastening.

Finishing touches

Bend your cat into shape. Cover the tail wire. Wind it around the skewer. Glue on the eyes, and the head if necessary.

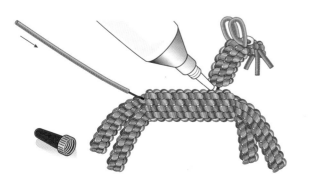

Animal parade

You will need...

- wire
- sewing thread
- toothpick
- scissors
- old scissors
- moving eyes
- glue

To make the lion:
- 45cm (18in) scoubidou threads: 8 orange threads, 1 yellow thread

To make the giraffe:
- scoubidou threads: 4 x 90cm (36in) orange and 4 x 90cm (36in) white threads; 1 x 45cm (18in) black thread

Lion

Paws and body

Cut 2 pieces of wire 10cm (4in) in length to reinforce the paws and an 8cm (3¼in) length to reinforce the body. Using the diagram as a guide, follow the same method as for the cat.

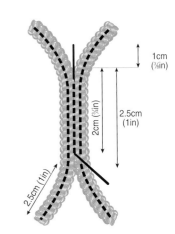

1cm (⅜in)

2.5cm (1in)

2cm (¾in)

2.5cm (1in)

Head

Weave a 6-strand spiral scoubidou over 1cm (⅜in), securing it as for the cat. To make the mane, thread pieces of 4cm (1½in) long yellow thread into each loop formed in the next 2 rows. Reduce your threads by 2 threads in the next row.

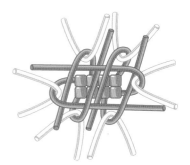

Ears

Make 2 loops in a 6cm (2⅜in) thread and secure them with sewing thread. Insert them into the next row. Continue weaving a round scoubidou over 1cm (⅜in), then finish with a rounded fastening.

Finishing touches

Bend the animal into shape. Even out the mane. Cover the tail wire. Bend the tail back and attach a piece of knotted thread. Glue on the eyes, then the head if necessary.

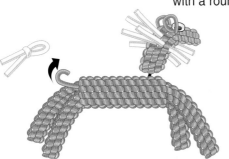

Giraffe

Hooves and body

Cut 2 x 14cm (5½in) lengths of wire to reinforce the hooves, and a 12cm (4¾in) length to reinforce the body. Using the diagram as a guide, follow the same method as for the cat.

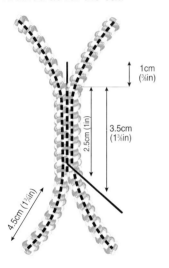

1cm (⅜in)

3.5cm (1⅜in)

2.5cm (1in)

4.5cm (1¾in)

Head

Weave a 6-strand spiral scoubidou over 4.5cm (1¾in), securing it as for the cat. While you are doing this, insert a 3cm (1⅛in) length of black thread into each row to make the mane, by passing it around the wire.

Reduce your threads by 2. Make the ears as for the lion but with a 7cm (2¾in) length of thread. In the next row, insert a 4cm (1½in) length of reinforced thread to make the horns. Weave a round scoubidou for 1cm (⅜in), then finish with a rounded fastening.

Finishing touches

As for the lion.

Animal parade

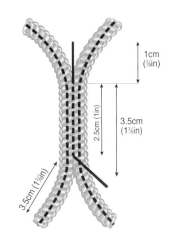

You will need...

- wire
- toothpick
- scissors
- old scissors
- moving eyes
- glue

To make the zebra:
- 90cm (36in) scoubidou threads, 4 black and 4 white

To make the elephant:
- 8 x 90cm (36in) scoubidou threads in grey; 1 x 45cm (18in) white thread and 1 x 45cm (18in) pink thread
- skewer

To make the tortoise:
- 45cm (18in) scoubidou threads, 8 bright green, 1 dark green, 1 yellow
- pen

Elephant

Feet and body
Cut 2 x 12cm (4¾in) lengths of wire to reinforce the feet and a 9cm (3½in) length to reinforce the body. Using the diagram as a guide, follow the same method as for the cat.

Head
Start with an 8-strand round reinforced scoubidou (with holding knot and 7cm/2¾in wire). At 0.5cm (³⁄₁₆in) make a hole with a toothpick then, 0.5cm (³⁄₁₆in) later, make another hole perpendicular to the first. Continue for 1cm (⅜in). Reduce your number of threads by 2 threads. Complete 2 rows then make a third hole parallel to the second. Complete another 2 rows. End with 4 threads over 3.5cm (1⅜in), then finish with a rounded fastening.

Finishing touches
Bend the scoubidou into shape. Reinforce a 38cm (15in) pink thread and a 36cm (14⅛in) white thread. Thread the first into the second hole in the head, then pass the second thread into the third hole. Cover any excess wire sticking out of the body. Apply a little glue to the base, thread it into the first hole in the head, then bend it back. Make tusks, ears and a tail. Glue on the eyes.

Zebra

Hooves and body

Cut 2 x 10cm (4in) lengths of wire to reinforce the hooves and an 8cm (3¼in) length to reinforce the body of the zebra. Using the diagram as a guide, follow the same method as for the cat.

Head

Weave a 6-strand spiral scoubidou for 2cm (¾in), securing it as for the cat. While you are doing this, insert lengths of black and white thread to make the mane, as for the giraffe. To make the ears, proceed as for the lion with a thread 8cm (3¼in) in length. Reduce your number of threads by 2 threads. Weave a round scoubidou for 1.5cm (⅝in), then finish with a rounded fastening.

Finishing touches

As for the lion.

Tortoise

Feet and body

Weave 2 bright green 4-strand round reinforced scoubidous (with holding knot and 8cm/3¼in wires) over 1cm (⅜in). Bring the two scoubidous together. Thread a new 7cm (2¾in) wire into the centre, leaving 1cm (⅜in) excess. Weave a rectangular scoubidou for 3.5cm (1⅜in). Revert to making 2 separate round reinforced scoubidous. Trim all threads.

Head

Weave a 4-strand round scoubidou for 1cm (⅜in), and secure it as for the cat. Finish with a rounded fastening.

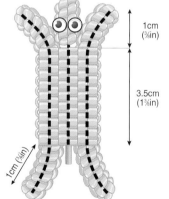

1cm (⅜in)

3.5cm (1⅜in)

1cm (⅜in)

Shell

Reinforce the 2 remaining threads. Starting at the centre of the shell, make circles in the dark green thread by wrapping it around a pen twice.

Make the edges of the shell from reinforced yellow thread, making a full loop around each circle. Secure the starting point with your final loop. Bend the shell into shape and glue it onto the body.

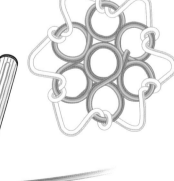

Keyring zing

You will need...
- moving eyes
- toothpick
- foam board
- wire
- old scissors
- scissors
- glue

To make the pig:
- 1 keyring
- scoubidou threads:
  4 x 90cm (36in) pink
  threads; 1 x 20cm (8in)
  pink thread
- black felt

To make the dog:
- 1 keyring (with clip
  attachment
- 90cm (36in) scoubidou
  threads: 3 white and
  2 black

Tip
Refer to pages 7 and 8
for help on making knots,
reinforcing, spacer rows
and finishing touches.

Pig keyring

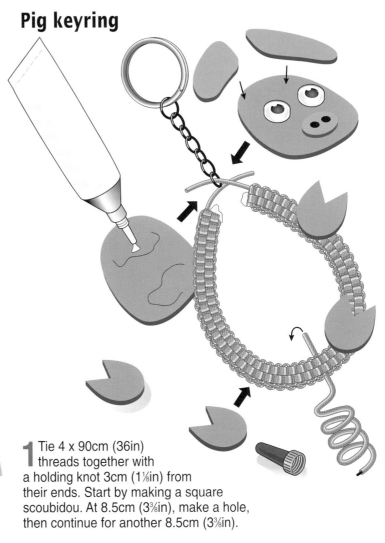

1 Tie 4 x 90cm (36in)
threads together with
a holding knot 3cm (1⅛in) from
their ends. Start by making a square
scoubidou. At 8.5cm (3⅜in), make a hole,
then continue for another 8.5cm (3⅜in).

2 At each end of the scoubidou, cut 3 out of the 4 threads.
Glue the ends to make a ring. Leave to dry. Attach the
keyring with the 2 remaining threads.

3 Reinforce the 20cm (8in) thread. Thread it into the hole
and bend it back. Twist it round using a pen.

4 Cut the head and trotters out of foam board (see the
templates at the back of this book). Glue together and
then add the eyes. Cut the nostrils out of black felt.

Dog keyring

1 Tie 2 black threads, 2 white threads, and a 22cm (8⅝in) length of wire together with a holding knot 1cm (⅜in) from their ends. Weave a round reinforced scoubidou for 10cm (4in). Make a hole then continue for 10cm (4in).

2 Trim the scoubidou threads close to your work at each end. Secure the wire to the keyring.

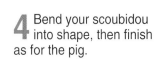

3 To make the tail, start off a round reinforced scoubidou, with a holding knot, for 3 rows. Thread the reinforced section into the body. Pass the threads either side and continue for 1.5cm (⅝in). Trim one of the threads close to your work. Continue with 3 threads over 1cm (⅜in).

4 Bend your scoubidou into shape, then finish as for the pig.

Martian buddies

You will need...

- moving eyes
- wire
- old scissors
- scissors
- glue

To make the Martian:
- light green and dark green scoubidou threads: 1 x 90cm (36in) and 1 x 45cm (18in) in each colour
- toothpick
- offcut of green foam board
- green beads: 1 bead 20mm (¾in) in diameter; 3 beads 10mm (⅜in) in diameter
- 1 pebble

To make the dog:
- light green and dark green scoubidou threads: 4 x 90cm (36in) in each colour
- green beads: 1 bead 20mm (¾in) in diameter; 1 bead 10mm (⅜in) in diameter

Template shown actual size

Martian

10cm (4in) · 6cm (2⅜in) · 1cm (⅜in) · 5mm (¼in) · 7cm (2¾in) · 5mm (¼in) · 1cm (⅜in)

Body

Start off a 4-strand square scoubidou with a hidden knot around a 22cm (8⅝in) length of wire with 6cm (2⅜in) excess. Weave for 10cm (4in), making holes (see p.8) as shown in the diagram, then stop. Line up the holes and bend the scoubidou. Apply a little glue to the ends. Insert 2 reinforced threads 16cm (6¼in) long into the holes. Bend them.

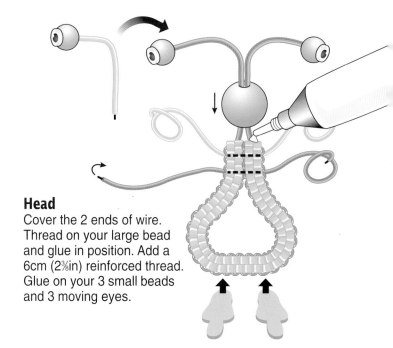

Head

Cover the 2 ends of wire. Thread on your large bead and glue in position. Add a 6cm (2⅜in) reinforced thread. Glue on your 3 small beads and 3 moving eyes.

Finishing touches

Glue on the feet, made from foam board, then glue the scoubidou onto the pebble.

Dog

Paws and body

Cut 2 x 12cm (4¾in) lengths of wire to reinforce the paws, and a 21cm (8¼in) length to reinforce the body. Using the diagram as a guide, proceed as for the cat on page 33, weaving square scoubidous.

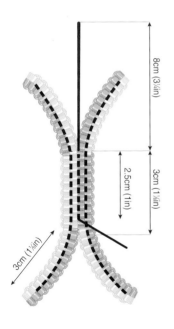

8cm (3¼in)

3cm (1⅛in)

2.5cm (1in)

3cm (1⅛in)

Finishing touches

Cover the ends of the body wire. To make the head, thread on your large bead. Thread in 2 reinforced threads (5cm/2in and 9cm/3½in). Glue the bead on. Bend the tail and ears. Glue on a small bead and a moving eye.

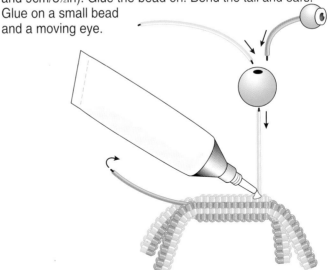

Fantasy beasts

You will need...

- wire
- old scissors
- scissors
- moving eyes

To make the snake:
- 90cm (36in) scoubidou threads: 4 orange, 2 yellow, 2 black, 2 grey, 2 green
- offcuts of foam board in green and red
- 2 white beads 10mm (⅜in) in diameter
- 1 small bell
- 1 stone or 1 pebble

To make the dragon:
- 90cm (36in) scoubidou threads: 8 yellow, 4 red, 3 green
- toothpick
- green beads: 2 beads 15mm (⅝in) in diameter; 2 beads 20mm (¾in) in diameter
- 1 small hairgrip for the mouth
- 1 plastic tube (optional)

Snake paperweight

1 Tie together 2 orange threads, 1 grey thread, 1 black thread, 1 green thread, 1 yellow thread and a 40cm (16in) length of wire with a holding knot 1.5cm (⅝in) from their ends. Weave a reinforced spiral scoubidou for 25cm (9⅞in).

2 Cut the green thread and the grey thread and make a 4-strand round scoubidou over 6cm (2⅜in). Reduce numbers by one orange thread and continue working with 3 threads until 1cm (⅜in) of wire remains.

3 At the tail end, cover the reinforcement. Knot the threads and trim to finish. Attach the small bell by bending back the wire.

4 At the head end, trim 4 threads close to your work and cut 2 threads to 1cm (⅜in). Cut the head and tongue out from foam board (templates at the back of this book). Stick the head onto the wire and glue it to the scoubidou. Glue down the tongue and the top of the head. Glue on the beads, then the moving eyes.

Finishing touches
Bend the snake into shape and glue it onto a stone.

Tip
Refer to pages 7 and 8. As you weave, replace threads that run out by adding new ones.

Fantasy beasts

Dragon

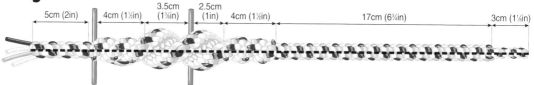

1 Tie 2 yellow threads, 1 red thread, 1 green thread, and a 40cm (16in) length of wire with a holding knot 1cm (⅜in) from their ends. Weave a round reinforced scoubidou over 5cm (2in).

2 Add 2 yellow threads. Complete 2 spiral rows. Make a hole by inserting a toothpick. Continue a spiral scoubidou for 4cm (1½in). Add 4 yellow threads and weave a spiral with all 10 threads over 3.5cm (1⅜in). Make a second hole. Continue the spiral for 2.5cm (1in).

3 Reduce the number of threads by 4 yellow threads and weave a spiral with the remaining 6 for 4cm (1½in). Reduce the number by another 2 yellow threads and weave a round scoubidou for 17cm (6¾in). Take off another yellow thread and weave a 3-strand scoubidou until you get to the end of the wire. Knot the threads and trim them close to your work.

4 Reinforce 2 red threads – one 43cm (17in) long for the front feet; one 46cm (18in) for the hind feet. Thread them into the holes, then thread on the beads. Starting with a hidden knot, weave 4-strand scoubidous onto the reinforced threads, for 1.5cm (⅝in) at the front and 3cm (1⅛in) at the back. Loop the feet.

5 Trim the starting threads and wire close to your work. Glue on the hairgrip. Reinforce 2 red threads 10cm (4in) in length and make 2 spirals for the horns. Glue them onto the hairgrip. Bend the dragon into shape.

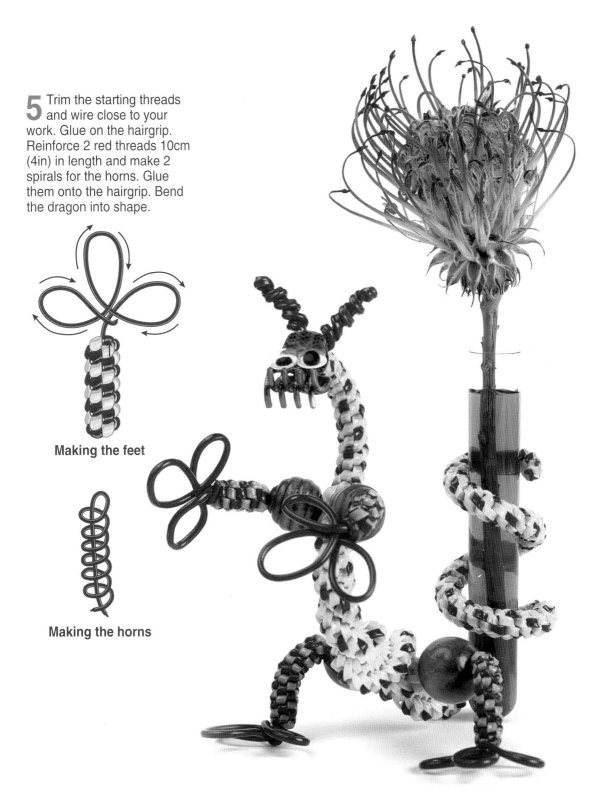

Making the feet

Making the horns

Templates

Party napkin rings
page 16

Pig keyring
page 38

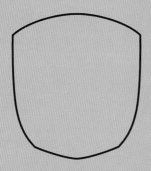

**Dog keyring
page 39**

**Snake paperweight
page 42**

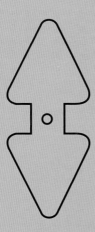